Gum Arabic

Alan Morrison

Cyberwit.net
HIG 45 Kaushambi Kunj, Kalindipuram
Allahabad - 211011 (U.P.) India
http://www.cyberwit.net
Tel: +(91) 9415091004 +(91) (532) 2552257
E-mail: info@cyberwit.net

Printed at Repro India Limited.

For Vanessa and Sam

By the same author

Shabbigentile
(Culture Matters, 2019)

Tan Raptures
(Smokestack Books, 2017)

Shadows Waltz Haltingly
(Lapwing Publications, 2015)

Odour of Devon Violet
(www.odourofdevonviolet.com, 2014)

Blaze a Vanishing and *The Tall Skies*
(Waterloo Press, 2013)

Captive Dragons/ The Shadow Thorns
(Waterloo Press, 2011)

Keir Hardie Street
(Smokestack Books, 2010)

A Tapestry of Absent Sitters
(Waterloo Press, 2009)

Picaresque
(chipmunkapublishing, 2008)

The Mansion Gardens
(Paula Brown Publishing, 2006)

Gum Arabic

Gum Arabic

'Populist politicians build their base by constructing an in-group —in this case, hardworking, white Britons—and pitching themselves as the champions of this "oppressed" group. They then blame the out-group—Muslims, migrants and scroungers—for the hardships every-one else is suffering'.

Grace Blakely, *The New Statesman* 14th August 2019

Daily he's cursing
Under hostile breath
At the ever-increasing
Numbers of turbans,
Hijabs, niqabs,
Burqas embarking
In dogwhistle-daylight
On his local high street -
"Bank robbers"
And *"letterboxes"*
He parrots the prime
Minister, for he's one
Of Boris's blue collars...

Does he ever think
As he takes a lick
Of the cigarette paper's
Seam of Gum Arabic
That his daily smoking
Habit is dependent
On acacia sap

Harvested in African
Islamic countries,
The Sudan, for instance,
Once a vast dusty
Theatre of war
In our far-flung
Colonial campaigns,
Pith-helmeted
Imperialist exploits,
Way back when
We fought hedged
In *zarebas*
Of thorn and scrub
In dusty squares
Awaiting the mass
Charge of Dervishes
In turbans and white
Robes, *jibbas*,
Patched with squares
And rectangles
Of various colours,
And the greased-haired
Hadendowa -
Rudyard Kipling's
'Fuzzy Wuzzy' -
Screaming towards us
In the name of the Mahdi
(Muhammad Ahmad
bin Abd Allah),
Kalifa, Osman Digna...

Not so far removed
From today, history

Repeating itself
Like a muttering
Old man, now foreign
Service helmets
Are a different shape
And camouflaged
As the uniforms from
Khaki to disruptive
Patterns, *daguet* fatigues,
But the principle is
Still the same, foreign
Interventions in
Sandy dominions
Against fearless
Insurgents fighting
For a Caliphate...

(As I write this
An American drone
Assassinates
Suleimani
And Mohammed
Ali Ebrahimi
Known by the *nom
de guerre* Abu
Mahdi al-Muhandis;
And all of this
Has an impact
Domestically...)

Does he think,
Does his subconscious
Cast back through

Ancestral memory
As he takes his
Daily lick
Of Gum Arabic...?

His daily hate is
Spoon-fed him
By the red top
Newspapers
Which smear his
Familiar enemies
Framed for him -
"Scroungers", immigrants,
Muslims, Gypsies,
"Corbynistas"
(There's no smoke
Without fire...) -
Make him hate them
Even more than
He hates himself,
His unaffordable
Life, his property-
Worship, his
Prostration before
Home ownership,
His fruitless pursuit
Of fulfilment
Through consuming,
For the red tops
Know if you throw
Enough mud some
Is bound to stick
Like Gum Arabic...

The Origami Man

I

He's scrunched up on the bench there most days
Under the heavy-sighing skies of Hove
On the pedestrian street, rapt in his art,
Craned on a bench –the crumpled man
Makes his creasing menageries of paper
Animals from different coloured bits of card;
Puddles for hissing ashtrays, oblivious
To his surroundings, the origami man's
Lost to the flow of his folding fingers,
Gnarled, tobacco'd to a scorched orange,
A bunch of grubby carrots freshly dug-up
(Every bit as nifty preparing his roll ups),
Grappling with the elements –his carrot-
Fingers fold and twist, triangulate
All manner of paper chimeras –Griffin,
Phoenix, Pegasus, Behemoth, Sphinx…

Time-bit tribulations have made this
Origami man, crinkled his skin
To folds and creases, whittled him down
To a glass-eyed gist, a clenched fist,
A gnarled knob of clay sculpted again
And again after fits of dissatisfaction
With its irregular shape; his droopy eyelids
Stung with disappointments to a dolphin's
Bulbous with dropsy; irises, scratched
Traceries of shattered aspirations;

Brown brow ploughed to furrows,
Brutalised arable, corrugated with flint…

Paper is malleable; he can manipulate it
Into whatever animal he desires,
Any shape he imagines; turn children's
Eyes for immanent moments before
They're distracted by plastic temptations,
Spiritless bric-a-brac staring absently
At them from cut-price displays –
But paper catches like nothing else can…

II

The crumpled genius of the origami man
Has captured itself in inscrutable snapshots
Of minors' future memories –his profitless
Gifts, his demonstrable craft, simple
And complex, unmarketable because
Authentic –the artisan's hex;
His customers are mostly penniless
Pigeons tapping their beaks on his paper birds,
Homing in on the coos of his stomach…

Time's hands have made the origami man
From paper not clay –he is origami-made,
More malleable that way, more easily
Discarded –crumpled Prometheus,
Pinched Sisyphus, he has the magic touch
With the pulp spoils of his deciduous
Substance: he alone can scrunch up the paper
If its shape dissatisfies him, then smooth it

Out on the ground, and start shaping
Another byzantine pavement creation…

III

But always there is progress lingering
At the dim margins of the origami man's mind,
Shadowing his pitch, so he keeps changing it
By simple paces, or sometimes more intrepid
Expeditions to far-flung benches, long-slogged
Campaigns of shuffling feet sockless
In burnt-rubber trainers punctured at the soles –
Inching thickly across a stretch of pavement-
Carpet in concrete slippers; and there
He'll decamp to damp his paper camels…

But still gossips of little birds ripple his ears
Like whispering Harpies: progress is limbering,
It threatens to usurp his purpose,
Make his special paper-craft obsolete,
So he is circumspect, suspicious;
And such origami angst wrings his rag-brow,
Scores more creases across its slowly
Traumatising eggshell-beige –for he knew
Now his paper-folding days were numbered,
Had been for some time, his hopes flapped
Down through the letterbox's burst brown study,
Those ominous ecru-coloured envelopes,
Policing correspondence apportioning
Punishments and sanctions as opposed
To providing support for the working poor,
The unemployed, incapacitated, or

Occupationally orphaned, tan paper
Rectangles, guillotined edge to edge, sealed
And gummed missives of Customer Compliance
From the Department for Wasting Paper –
Reprimands and threatening gestures
Of the Government's malignant origami…

But more was to come: the game-changing
Range of new technology: three-dimensional
Printers that can make automatic plastic
Sculptures, not of animals or mythical
Creatures, but guns and things, no skill
Involved of course in this fingerless origami,
Now the middle man was cut out of the craft,
And images could now be made tangible,
With triggers, weaponised thoughtforms:
A killer origami –being a natural luddite,
A diehard proponent of the simple hand-
Folding technique, he knew what he would do
If he ever got his magic hands on one of those
Pernicious contraptions of origami sacrilege,
He'd put the plastic barrel to his head
And fold its trigger, no *entfremdung* for him:
Sooner bite the cartridge of oblivion…

IV

On a listless spring Sunday I saw him haunting
That brittle bench again, but this time,
No crumpled paper animals were on display
Sparring inanimately at his muttering feet:

Now, his melted shoes were welded to
An oily cloth on which motley jumbles
Of manufactured four-legged miniatures
Congregated, cast-offs from a refurbished
Charity shop, glazed china animals
Honeyed in ambers of hoary afterglows,
And coated in dusts of mothballed
Grandmothers' sideboard reliquaries,
Kitsch Seventies' souvenirs, now chic…

I picked and inspected a tacky mock-Regency
Porcelain Spaniel –possibly worth something,
Or just a second look– and placed a quid in
The origami man's half-bandaged hand,
Palm blackened as a collier's, thumb
Ochred, grey wisps of crinkling smoke
Tapering from a crumpled rollup gripped
In his singed fingers; then he reached for
A tiny gold-brown Labrador, its flambé
Glaze now caramelising like heated Demerara,
And placed it in my palm, no doubt not wanting
To be characterised as a 'charity case' –

I asked rhetorically: *You're normally
The origami man, aren't you?* His pale
Eyes of yolky albumen, like two poached
Quail's eggs, glistened up –*That's right,*
He mumbled glumly, *But it's too windy
For paper gifts today: they'd blow away…*

V

One day I noticed his miniature bestiary
Of mythical paper creatures scattered
Round an empty bench –the origami
Man nowhere in sight… Had the crumpled-
Up man simply blown away, or had
He transmogrified into origami myth…?

The Blue, the Gray and the Brown

It crouches in terracotta Gothic behind
The charcoal arteries of leafless trees,
· Its rocketing spires copper-plated in something between
Mint, mantis and Paris green –
Inside its entrance stand paneled doors of slate gray,
Wooden obelisks whispering of entranceways,
Rococo moldings, baroque launches
Of intricately decorated vaulted ceilings
Veined with French rose and Thulian pink,
And writhing with tapering curlicues and vine-like
Arabesques encircling archipelagos
Of flowered crosses and yellow roses –
Faintly resembling English Tudor blooms –
I pause for some time, my eyes poring over
The unexpected prettification of this church,
This empty chapel, attempting to fathom
The blossoming obsessions of shrubs,
Luscious traceries and floral labyrinths –
Such natural patterning has subtly enchanted
The Lutheran stone of this Protestant sepulchre,
This Nordic Christian reliquary…
                              A service
Has just finished –traditionally ill-attended–
And pockets of parishioners shuffle out from
The main chapel, women and children returning
Outside to the secular daylight of Sweden,
Having verified their salvations within…

Vacated, I trip in and straight onto gray
And black chequered tiles, struck by the launch

Of the aisle up to a glowing candelabrum
Hanging before a distant altar –icily distant;
Stood to each side, blue-gray and cornflower
Shelves lined with unopened prayer books –
A pace forwards, I stop to study the decorous
Pew-ends of carved Lancet arches painted
Davy's gray over panels of sky-blue,
And Elcho-coloured kneeling cushions combing
Smooth timberwolf pews… then up to
The pulpit adorned with sculpted saints and scribes!
Gowned in gray, taupe and terracotta,
Mounted in arches of silver-gray wood,
Gold haloes for headrests; near to them,
A Modernist wooden slate-gray organ looms!
Complementarily to the other side
Like a slatted Menhir with rows of black-gapped
Shining white teeth, and peddle-feet;
But the true centrepiece, illumined by
A backdrop bay of seven stained glass windows:
A stunning altar enclosed within a knee-high
Gray fortress of wood-pillared gating,
Lined with mouse-brown cushions for knees and elbows –
Christ and His Saints glancing down from painted panels
Arced in baroque spires like a decorative
Wedding cake stacked with greying icing…

How is it that this spectacle of subtle blues,
Browns, fauns and many shades of gray
Can seem and feel at once so colourful, uplifting,
Light-full and free of all the stony gloom and shadowy,
Echoey, colourless austereness of those tortured
Little churches back in my distant damp country…?

And why paint a chapel gray as if to capture
Qualities of stone when all the walls
And furnishings are carved from wood? But then,
The inkling of a Christian still clinging in me
Tugs at my sleeve, like a child, and whispers simply,
These are the stony tones of faith's simplicity,
Christianity is cloaked in psychical
Chiaroscuro –besides, John Calvin
Would have disapproved, and Martin Luther
Would have proscribed richer spectrums as sinful,
Lapses of taste into temptation, approved
Only the puritanical, even though there is,
Nonetheless, something refulgent about these
Numinous greys and subtle blues;
A boreal sensibility, a Nordic predilection…

For they do say that Odin when in human form
With his long white beard straggly as Yggdrasil's
Tangled roots wore a long gray gown
And tall pointed hat of flopping sky-blue felt,
Gnarled brown staff in hand, the Psychopompos
Prototype of Tolkien's Gandalf the Gray –
And so blues, greys and browns would appear
To be the main mythological hues,
The dreamed shades of otherworldly figures,
Whether old Norse Gods, Yahwehs or wizards…

Summer Without Monika

The cancer has crept up through her lungs like acrid damp
After forty-odd years on sixty fags a day,
Her emphysema-hampered lungs have long been wrung
By choking pistons of cigarettes and now she
Wants to fade away for there's not much fun in life
When every hour is a fight for breath, the itch on
The tongue still ignited by the thought of a lighted cigarette
In spite of there being so little in her air-pumps left
To appreciate the drag and pout, the luxurious smoke,
The sting of nicotine, tickle of tar at the back of the throat –
Everything nostalgic is brocaded in tobacco…

She's nearly delirious now, still chimneying away
As she gasps for breath, and her memory's dismembering –
She never learnt to speak chic English like the rest
Of her aspiring generation of Swedes, and yet,
Apparently, this afternoon she started singing songs
In perfect English, lyrics she'd not learnt consciously,
In a foreign language strange to her ears which sounds
To Swedes as if it swallows the ends of its words,
Now she speaks it, spins it into music, her scorched
Ochre fingertips accompanying on air-piano–
A mystery fluency perhaps sourced from her smoky
Unconscious now suddenly unchained, catching on her
Enchanted tongue just as soon to learn in any case
The lingua franca of absence, stubbed out in an ashtray…

Antimacassar

My father grey and crumpled in his armchair
Scrunched-up like a discarded newspaper,
Or a sad clown reflecting on a vague despair –
Ash-skinned, all smoke, bones and memories, fogged glare,
A singed antimacassar still hanging in there…

Carnation Stains

My past is a lineage of absent goodbyes:
Old gnarled friendships forged from roots
Of accident and circumstance, essential, resentful,
Ripped out by change's grab, torn up –
Never revisited; violent early loves,
Once everything and nothing at once; absolute;
Gone sudden as first unflinching fires –
From thorny togetherness to brutal oblivion,
Not even the closure of a final parting touch,
No more in touch –but haunted by
A thought's receding clutch...

Now –only now– aware my mother's gourd
Has long been scoured through this corroding
Disease diagnosed only after the greater part of her
Had gone in all but name and body, bar
Fractured stares of recognition, rinsed tears
Staining like rain on the shapeless pasture of her
Pale green jumper, blotting to tiny carnations;
Vague glimmers of how she was an agony ago
In a cottage's glooms; she'd waited so long,
Through vicissitudes of poverty and nerves,
Just for her soul's imago to spin back to
Caterpillar inhibitions –fate's last insult,
More shattering than traumas that brought her to
This grotesque metamorphosis –part Pinocchio,
Part mule, *eeyore-eeyore*– this winding down,
This packing up of things, components of her
Robbed *who*, her core, her *ego*, personality,

Pinhead spark of eye that flexes until
The spirit trips the light... She waits still,
Without time, without appointment, her
Vim undiminished, still implicit in each twitch
Of limb, even in her stillness, in this fug
Of Bognor and chronic bronchitis...

Jogged back to powerless present-sense
Of jammed motor, sudden mortal jolt to symbolic
Bowls of mushy solids, flagons of thickened fluids,
Dignity-stripping damp patches staining her
Numb underside, brutal betrayal of elasticated
Trousers to a travesty of trunks;
Then the howl of recognition –the howl
Of her soul, the thunderous sob of her soul,
The harrowing wail and plaintive whine –
A marsh-warbler's shuddering cry –
Its trembling refrain like an agonised child
Abandoned by softer certainties,
Sympathies and parents, finally ending in
A strangled pitch like the little girl she once was,
Still is, trapped in a mass of twitching muscles
And acid reflux, no redux, all corroding…

That sound –scissoring through any soul I might house;
Sound of a soul torn out in torment,
Amplified by jungles of phlegm, scrubs of mucus,
Ectoplasms sculpting themselves in her
Un-witnessed chest –now I hear it in everything:
The piping, spine-pitched squeak of a rusty door-hinge;
Perambulating ambulance sirens;
Shrieks of night-startled seagulls;
Washing machines screeching into spins –

Then thinning, thinning into faint quavers
Of a trampled bantam –that quailing pause
Before its tortured crescendo tears
Through the ears: a quaking adult-child's...

This scourge is worse than all those winters
Of stomach-cramping fasts in that cottage-carcass,
That crooked, crouching, neurotic cottage
Of cobwebbed nooks' arachnid caryatids,
Crumpled husks coiled like locks of tobacco,
In that jarred hamlet of browning nostalgia,
Where she began vanishing into a vaguer shade...

And –as I didn't say goodbye to our root-house,
Our neglected grotto, our half-renovated
Hovel of enervated nerves, phantom-memories,
That rambling patch of our rusticated making,
Where my soul was grown in mushroom-glooms
Together with obsessions sprouting horns
Rapacious as damp's buff funguses
Spawning Lilliputian trumpets on phantasmal walls –
Another damp pattern's staining later in
To mouldering adulthood, spattering
Into tiny carnation stains: I've missed, again,
My chance to say goodbye to *her*, to *who* she was,
That feisty rose who somehow bloomed
From gloom-plunged balconies of a concrete
Sink estate into one of time's unnoticed
Miracles I *know* I witnessed and *in* whom
I must believe –as Hell is the absence of God,
And Heaven the presence of everything loved–
To leave room for doubt so faith can flower
Once carnation stains fade out...

Brambling Damp Rampant

...the children pointed out there were some flowers on the wall...I went in the front room, and sure enough it was. It wasn't flowers, it was fungus. In fact, it was toadstools, big ones too. About two inches in diameter. ...So we plucked these toadstools off the wall...

'Toadstools in the Parlour', 'Industrial Slums', *No Place Like Home – Britain's Housing Tragedy*, Frank Allaun (Andrew Deutsch, 1972)

The occurrence of damp through condensation in the home is often aesthetically objectionable and by virtue of fungi and black stains on the walls. It is also practically difficult to live with when bed-clothing and bed linen become damp, and when leatherware and articles of clothing in cupboards become green-mouldy and ruined...

'High, damp and mouldy', *No Place Like Home – Britain's Housing Tragedy*, Frank Allaun (Andrew Deutsch, 1972)

This is the dragon's day, the devourer's:
Orders are given to the enemy for a time
With underground proliferation of mould.
With constant whisper and with casual question,
To haunt the poisoned in his shunned house

W.H. Auden, '1929'

All English sing along to an orchestra of damp!
A whispering symphony of mould spores! Behold
The gnomic song of the laughing damp, the sobbing mould!
O those invisible microbes that take hold on the lungs

From young ages, cling like lichen to the bronchia,
Little black implacable specks which so nostalgically
Coagulate in the trachea, turn to oily curds
In the air-tubes as soot once did in barrel chests
Of chimney sweeps, or coal dust in hacking
Pit-shaft coughs of spluttering miners, or charcoal
Resins in the churning black catarrhs –black as
Weepers on pallbearers' heads– of char ladies
Disguising bouquets of blood and sweat behind
Patchouli oil that smells of mould and mildew,
A damp spice for bohemians, hippie-perfume,
Composite of compost and pot –O all those slogging
Trades long abolished but now on the brink of coming
Back –while the ancestral British stain of damp
Has never really gone away, only faded for a time
Under the damp-coat, and so we keep up our
National traditions of asthma, emphysema
And rattling chests (while tuberculosis
Is breaking out again, recrudescent through
Ghettoised lodgings, overcrowded digs,
Temporary accommodation, garden sheds)
Into the new era of under-consumption in spite
Of over-production, borderline consumption
And sputum-productive coughs –and we have the damp
To thank for that, the creeping damp, the darkly
Laughing damp and the blackly sobbing mould
That bruises on our poorly insulated walls,
Glistening filigrees like mollusc spoors, shiny,
Wet, black damp and blue mould our slummy
Private landlords tell us we can simply patch up
With a spot of paint, or wipe off with a damp cloth –
How's that? Damp will wipe away damp...?

So here's to sanguine Stainand colours & rebatements of Old

England: brambling damp rampant, grimpant green, black &
blue mould

The damp is implacable, once it takes hold
Of the lungs it never completely clears,
But amplifies mucus and catarrhs to crowing orchestras,
Clamps itself like moss against the lung-linings,
Creeps up through time, when we least expect it to resurface –
Recrudescent slime– to reassert its hoary hold,
Its stubborn mould, like a musty old religion,
Ignored but never quite forgotten, never letting us forget it,
Resurgent in a churning cough, biliously productive,
Glutinous deposits of phlegm and mucus, thick
And slimy as frogspawn or algae gunk in a fish tank –
We have the English damp to thank for that,
The moisture of our waterlogged country, our damp
Slushy island, and for the damp we have the rain
To thank, as well as porous houses specially
Constructed to be unfit for long-term habitation
And to structurally break out in cold sweats,
Until we find we pay far more than our unregulated
Rents for the privilege of shelter: we also pay with
Our wheezing chests, our health on shorthold tenancy,
Our lungs wrung out by sponging cowboy-goblins…

So here's to sanguine Stainand colours & rebatements of Old

England: brambling damp rampant, grimpant green, black &
blue mould

Damp apartments, mouldy studio flats, squats, bedsits,
Garrets, slums and hovels, all so many narrow houses

For our spluttering sojourns in partitioned towns
And ring-fenced cities, labyrinths of buy-to-lets,
For there's much profit to be made from damp,
Much capital-accumulation from mould spores,
Sealed in Chinese boxes of stucco-crumbling maisonettes
Not so much spirit-levelled as split-levelled with
Spittle-thin partitions dividing between phlegm-
Green and mucus-yellow, all damp simply painted
Over with only one coat of neutral tone, just a lick
Of paint… The damp is always with us, it never leaves us,
Accumulates on the mould-blotched walls of our
English lungs, our bronchial heritage, we island-
Stranded sputtering grampuses –sometimes rinses
Itself out through our throats when we're abroad in
Sunnier climes, taking our cures, or simply in better-
Insulated apartments on the Continent, particularly
Scandinavian –in Sweden, no mould spores can breed
In the ambient temperatures kept up in homes
Throughout the year for there's insufficient moisture
In the air for them to get a grip on any wall or ceiling –
To the Swedes, damp is something that died out
Long ago, it was vanquished along with slums,
Consumption, rickets, Christianity, and slavery,
With the epic settlement of social democracy;
Damp is something almost ancient, barbaric,
Unacceptably abject, damp is anathema to modern
Standards of basic health and wellbeing and how
Humanity must live if it is to survive the scourge
Of its own avoidable privations, its harvested
Allergens, its ancestral asthmas; damp is as much
A moral scandal to the Swedes as is asbestos
To the British (only latterly considered thus,
While damp is somehow still tolerated by us,

As if from some strange nostalgia, pathological lag,
Masochistic nostalgia, elemental sentimentalism,
And still private slumlords are under no prosecutable
Onus to stamp it out in the shoddy toadstool-
Sprouting properties they rent out so ruinously,
To cripple and asphyxiate our airways incrementally,
They tell us to mop up the damp with damp
Sponges while they mop up profits from our rents…

So here's to sanguine Stainand colours & rebatements of Old

England: brambling damp rampant, grimpant green, black &
blue mould

In spite of social progress through the ages,
Sometimes tortoise-slow, slug-slow, sluggish, tergiant,
Begrudging, the green-mouldy damp is always with us,
The gradualist damp that gathers in fungal aggregates
And accumulates through decades contrapuntal
In its toadstool bugles, its slimy fungus-trumpets,
Trumpets in the parlour –Ha! Ha! Catarrh
And rattling coughs among damp trumpets!–
Its vambraced brassart accompaniments, brass
Orchestras, the damp sprouts its' trumpeting
Vamplets, horns and flowers, flowers and horns,
To the brassier assertions that abject poverty
Has been incrementally eliminated through
The long plodding uphill slopes of traipsing epochs –
So Lettings Tsars tell us; but all the while wheezing
Progress follows progress, growth, growth, mould-
Growth, dry-rot, damp and mould continue
To sculpt their impasto of bronchial-spotting
Spoors and lung-tugging intaglio –and this is due

To the cowboy-botching British surface-wipe
Of social reforms that historically took off
The symptoms with wet cloths, while hoping
The structural faults of water-logging porous
Brickwork would somehow trickle down and drain away,
Dissipate and fade like the faint summer phantom
Of damp-stain patched up with a spot of paint
To turn to snowy powder by the following winter,
Wet hoarfrost that comes off on the fingers –or,
To simply take a wet cloth to the poor and wipe
Them off the map of damp walls! But the structural
Fault remains, that of stratification, until, today,
Dragging its reptile heels up the crumbling
Embankment, up the slippery escarpment
Of the twenty-first century's cusp, damp is
As much a part of Britishness as milk in tea,
Bacon and eggs, warm beer, cricket, biscuits, bronchitis…

So here's to sanguine Stainand colours & rebatements of Old

*England: brambling damp rampant, grimpant green, black &
blue mould*

We wean our children on the damp, succour
Them on mould, rear them in moist atmospheres
Unsalted –unlike their tears– until they take
The weight of waterlogged lungs, two porous
Foamy pails of water, Jack and Jills of rag-bunged
Pipes and overspills, and take laboured breaths
For tightening bronchial tubes; asthma,
Which the Romans termed *"rehearsal for death"* –
A traversal of heavy breath– bequeathed
To generations of children from poorest households,

An ancestral affliction, an ancient tradition
Of air-contraction, part of what makes us British,
While the damp itself was partly what finally
Repelled the Romans from crawling any higher
Up the brittle vertebra of Britain, beyond
The winding stone teeth of Hadrian's Wall;
Damp, implacable accompaniment to
The muggy island climate, can be patched up
With wallpaper –the yellower and mustier
The better– but its stain is textural, leaves
Impressions in air pockets and floral blisters,
As if to brocade it into embossed fungal murals,
A yellow, musty, creeping wallpaper all its own,
Dankly lustrous in scrolling mantle and foliating
Damp-lambrequins; or it can be coated over
With many licks of paint, mucus-yellow again,
Or magnolia, or phlegm-green are the most
Effective tones employed in its camouflaging;
And, as hardier perennials reared to grey-green
Toadstool cornets sprouting on dripping walls
By their beds, damp is something commonplace
And perfectly compatible with growth, phlegm-
Green shoots –for some of these baby boomers
Imbibed bucketfuls of the stuff in their infant years –
Along with asbestos– and are among those
Who advise a swift wipe with a cloth to sort it,
Take off all the frowsty powdery blacking
As if polishing leather boots with lampblack
From a tin –damp is a British tradition;
Or simply to leave our windows open allowing
Better ventilation, air-circulation, letting those
Draughts we traditionally try to insulate ourselves
Against with all manner of paraphernalia

From taping up windows or lining them
With sealing wax, grouting round sprouting
Trumpets of fungal fauna, insulating gaps under
Doors with draught-excluders, putting in newspaper
Lining under wallpaper, or opting for default
Thermals, extra rugs and carpets, woolly throws,
Electric blankets, thermal vests, prickling long johns,
Water bottles, plenty of jumpers; after all,
Some of them remind us, they grew up without
Any central heating, just heaped on plenty
Of blankets and jumpers to keep them warm in bed
At night, woke up in freezing winter mornings
To wash their faces in goose-bumping wash-basins,
Brush petrified teeth, scrape ice off frozen windows…

So here's to sanguine Stainand colours & rebatements of Old

*England: brambling damp rampant, grimpant green, black &
blue mould*

Damp is an English disease, along with gingivitis,
Status anxiety, asthma, one-upmanship, property-
Worship, depression, obsessional neurosis,
Seasonal affective disorder, compassion fatigue,
Chronic scroungerphobia, morbid sublimation
Of individuality and authentic personality
For bovine vicarious individualism through
Dog-like adoration of royalty, footballers,
Celebrities, imbeciles… The Swedes have damp-
Proofed houses properly insulated, kept at
Ambient temperatures, a comprehensively
Implemented social democracy, equality,
Lagom (*"just enough"*, *"everything in moderation"*),

Samforstånd, (*"mutual understanding"*), a fully
Functioning and less punitive welfare state
Or *Folkhemmet* (*"people's home"*); while we
English have the Welfare Hate and Thatcheritic
Attitudes towards the poor, unemployed,
Dispossessed, homeless, physically incapacitated
And mentally afflicted, and all victims of others'
Inveterate acquisitiveness –Calvinistic diets
Of *"deserving/undeserving"* dualisms;
The Swedish have *folkhemmet, lagom* and *samforstånd* –
The English have one-upmanship, damp, diazepam…

So here's to sanguine Stainand colours & rebatements of Old

England: brambling damp rampant, grimpant green, black &
blue mould

The English have the damp and the damp has the English
In its stranglehold of dark ancestral mould,
Its spores of microscopic black dandelion-clocks
Choking us slowly O so slowly as we rock our
Children in damp cots, woken up to churning coughs,
Concertina wheezes, chests fluttering with crows
And rooks, crows and rooks, for we're a race
Of crooks who con ourselves, scour ourselves
Out with spores from damp wallpaper, dust-trap
Carpets, thick pile, musty rugs, mouldy books
Clothbound and tumid *–O just wipe the damp away*
With a damp cloth and then the wall is spotless,
Or patch it up with a spot of damp-proof paint,
At least for a little time until the black damp
Creeps back every autumn and winter, thickening
In throttlång spring when the spores are interspersed

With pollen and pollutants; round the maypole,
Spores will sing Ring-a-ring-a-roses, a pocketful
Of mouldy spores, *atishoo, atishoo,* we all crawl down,
Ding-a-ling, in a miasma of damp and moulding,
This demi-parasite just off the coast of Europe,
This phlegm-green gem set in a distempered sea,
A mould-grey sea, under wet slate sky of wrung-
Dishcloth clouds, we're never dry, not in this
England so smitten with its cramped dampness…

So here's to sanguine Stainand colours & rebatements of Old

England: brambling damp rampant, grimpant green, black &
blue mould

And the damp is a class thing: an almost imperceptible
Biological weapon surreptitiously deployed
By the upper powers of our dampocracy,
Kleptocratic because it steals our health, silent
But deadly, our dank and rainy climate's special
Punishment for its poor, the musty-scented, over-
Ventilated invisible airborne invasion force
That shoots out spores from ventilation shafts
Of the impoverished, the *"undeserving poor"*
Deserving only mould-spores, the *"Council House*
And Violent-s" (*CHAVs* –from *charva*, Roma for
"Feral child"), travellers, squatters, *"scroungers"*,
"Spongers", damp *WRAGs*, quixotic tramps,
Mad hatters swinging willingly round lampposts
Tipsy on the spilt port of poor life choices,
All the flotsam of the great unwashed –the damp's
Their slow-creeping incremental population cap,
Asthmatic cramp, demographic clamp, demotic stamp,

Atmospheric pincer-movement on their capacity
To breathe unobstructedly; yes, damp-caused
Asthma is a gift for Malthusians, as dry-rot is
For Tories –implacable blue lambrequins,
Dexters of Torch-carrying escutcheons –emblems
Of implausibly disguised Mendelisms; damp
Marks parameters of class, sprouting truncheons;
Damp's the vitality-sapper of the poor,
And stains them with its stigma –all democracies
Should have compassion graphs measured by
The accumulative amount of damp and mould
Growing vertiginously on slum-walls of the poorest
Households, all that's worst about the English
Cannot be simply wiped away with a damp cloth,
But will always remain as long as the damp
Permeates –the mantle, pelmet and lambrequin
Of England is *brambling damp rampant…*

So here's to sanguine Stainand colours & rebatements of Old

England: brambling damp rampant, grimpant green, black &
blue mould…

Nasturtiums

for V.S.

They used to say *"be nasty to nasturtiums"*
For these flashing red and orange flowers thrive on neglect,
Blossom hardily in dry soil with little watering –
Except as comes naturally with noncommittal rain;
Unsociable but boldly coloured, growing on their own
(No commingling except with unassuming weeds)
Especially well when picked and arranged in a vase –
Nasturtiums have been known to drink water so fast
That other flowers bunched with them wilt from thirst,
But this is no malice, more a clumsiness, a quirk,
An unintended consequence from brutalising bloom;
Nasturtiums are the ruffians of flowers, harsh
But beautiful, indefatigable, self-reliant, tough
But fragile, as glass, monstrously sensitive
To unfamiliar comforts– with little nurturing
They grow up to expect nothing, are wise in
Their distrust of fuss, fragrances and strangers;
They suffer for their feistiness but are successful
At flourishing where other plants wither –for
They know nothing but harsh environments,
Are most at home in inhospitable beds; bashful
Flowers; cautious, hyper-vigilant, they mostly
Dread the wind that shudders through their petals,
Though this shuddering's disguised behind carefree façades;
A fundamental guardedness camouflaged against
The greenest gardens, lushest foliage –of all
Flowers nasturtiums are the most traumatised...

Hope at the Umpteenth Attempt

for V.S.

Hope is the hardest thing for you to bear
Because its empty promises are impossible
To put aside, and each time they inescapably
Collapse and the consequences escalate,
And the residue surges under the surface,
A tension that must be vented through
Unpredictable outbursts and precisest cutting:
Up on the surface these tensions rupture
Into rusty scrawls across scrolling across
Your olive skin, alphabetical cuts spelling
THIS IS HELL in a bloody marbling,
A message screaming grotesque cries for help;
And yet I've come to recognise that *HELL*
Is somewhere you know well and have grown
Accustomed, and that at least it doesn't
Disappoint you, doesn't build up your hopes
To let them down, doesn't promise you
Impossible things as glimpsed in dreams,
Ambitions, aspirations, wishes, phantasms,
Figments; for all of its prolific and horrific
Faults and afflictions, Hell is at least what
It says it is on the tin, doesn't pretend
Otherwise, doesn't fake kindness –kindness
That's actually sadism flimsily disguised
Like razor blades in tissue... and once you
Inscribed *SCROUNGER* on your forearm
When through incapacity you were unemployed

And were made to feel a burden on the state
Even though you received nothing from it
Because you had not then attained *"settled
Status"* and endured hostile attitudes from
Xenophobic neighbours who presumed you
Were Muslim, emboldened by immigrant-baiting
Tabloids tub-thumping for *"Brexit"* amid
The *"national self-harm"* of the referendum
After a decade of brutalising cuts...; those
Crisscrossing cuts pinking to scars, raised
Like nettle-rash brocading your luminous
Underarms, trespass upon your once-sacred
Bruise of a tattoo superimposing *HOPE*
As an inky poultice upon hopeless scars –
A permanent but impotent spell woven over
The veins of your wrist blurred under the skin
Like wires in milk blueing, bruising;
I can only hope that you'll resist the urge
To sever that word you've come to curse
As inherently cruel, can only hope you'll
Not snip through that precious word you despise,
But that you'll learn to let go of the pain
And anger, again, and again, delegate the rage
To a future day, not anticipate it too hastily,
At least appreciate *'to heal'* as a hypothetical
Concept, and, after pause for breath, pre-empt
Disappointment –make an umpteenth attempt…

The Lady in the Cabinet

for V.S.

I gave you *The Yellow Wallpaper* to read –
About a woman who imagines another woman
Trapped behind the walls of an attic bedroom
Sequestered for a quaintly termed *'rest cure'*
From her *'temporary nervous depression'*;
A woman trapped in the patterns of a damp attic's
Musty sulphur wallpaper; I suppose part
Of my hope in bringing you here to this quiet
Thirties-built rented maisonette was to help you
Heal, take *your 'rest cure'*, but there's no real
Cure for the years of abuse you endured
That seem unreal as bad dreams, nor for the drip-
Drip residue that endures ever since and leaves
A mustardy aftertaste, a sting in everything,
Reverberating to numbness on your tongue
Whenever you attempt to articulate anything
Relating to it, verbally relive it in alternative
Versions trying to find one which the soul-moving-
On can almost-accommodate; the chronic
Psychical scars that can only be patched up;
The punishing repeated lashes of flashback;
The scratching rut of trauma; the mental stains
That catch on fabrics of the present, tarnishing
All textures, scratching and scarring them…
After clawing halfway through Charlotte Perkins
Gilman's unsettling tale (almost a prose poem
On menopause warped, phantasmagorical Gothic-

Psychological allegory -O how grotesquely
Inadequate these hermeneutical terms
Just as those psychiatric plaster phrases applied
To your scars -*'emotionally unstable personality
Disorder'*- terms that trap us behind nursery bars,
Or brocaded wallpaper creeping with damp
And blotchy with mould spores, bloated with dust
And moisture, an appalling poultice pressed
Against our lips, smothering our mouths, or,
Salted, wrapped around your red-scarred arms),
You latching on particularly to that part
Depicting the wallpaper patterns as tangents
Plunging into nothingness, hurling themselves
Off their own scrolled edges, committing
Suicides in curlicues (metaphorically speaking,
Of course), but then abruptly truncating it,
Partly for lack of concentration, partly for it
Being written in your third language –after German,
Arabic– and pitched in baroquely expressed
Maple-dripped prose so typical of Yellow
Nineties literature (the Mauve Decade in Gilman's
America), cryptic turns of phrase, you spoke
About *"The lady" you* saw who was *"trapped"*
Inside the wooden cabinet I'd bought from
A charity shop to house my accidental collection
Of porcelain miniatures, refugee figurines –
Cheap replica Furstenberg, Meissen, chipped
Serendipities; you spoke of how the lady was
Menacing, of how she faintly knocked on the cabinet's
Glass at night, wanting you to let her out; so,
Draping the throw from the couch over the cabinet
At least kept her strange gray face from sight,
Although you'd still hear her tapping faintly on

The glass in spite, a faint knocking slightly
Muffled through the woollen throw; then when
I asked you to explain in what sense you *"saw"*
A lady in the cabinet you said you *"saw her"*
In your *"mind"* and that she was you, not your
Reflection, a nocturnal doppelganger with
Independent spontaneous expressions, trapped
Behind the glass, trapped inside the cabinet of your mind,
As if you were on display, confined,
A rigid figurine in your own right, reified –
Yet it felt cheapening putting it in such a figure
Of speech, a pathetic attempt to capture spiritual
Disfigurement… In spite of how deeply I pitied
Your difficult tilt of mind, tried to help you catch
The pieces of your splintered consciousness,
How much I sympathised, how my heart broke
Like the Gothic wooden clock you bought me for
My bereft birthday that dark summer plunged
Under shadowy boughs of dark thoughts,
Black leaves of bereavement, stung until numbed
By nettled nerves, festering mental burns
Of a breakdown which shook me to the core,
The broke clock whose pendulum just couldn't keep
A soft enough rhythm to sustain its rusty swing,
Its' brittle rocking, still echoing… faintly knocking…
I couldn't help appreciating the metaphor…

The Smiling Lady

You'd missed your medication for some days
But only just let me know, though I could tell
Something was amiss from the flushed look on your face
And by how your chocolate brown pupils seemed
To be melting into themselves, seemed mistier,
Chalkier, that you were being besieged by
Those invisibles only audible to you, verbal
Berserkers rebounding round your inner-ear,
Aural Furies, shell-like Harpies, which sound to you
As if external but are your own worst thoughts
Amplified, crowding round the tympanic cavities,
Echoes on the ossicles, taunting and tormenting you...

But then your attention switched to a crumpled
Old lady on a bench nearby who was struggling
To stretch a plastic bag over a filing box she'd
Bought, and you suggested that maybe I should
Go over to her see if she needed any help... As
I asked her, her cloudy pale gray eyes lit up
With sunlight almost childlike as a warm smile
Glowed buttercup-under-chin-golden across
Her soft wrinkly face stippled with little white
Tufts of hair like shreds spun from dandelion-clocks,
As she answered *Oh thank you, thank you so much...*
Good deed done, back in my cafe chair I noticed
How your own face had lit up, as you said:
Ah, she's smiling -I turned to see, *No, not at you,*
You continued, *She's just sat there... smiling...*
Smiling to herself... And sure as eggs is eggs

There was the frail old lady straightening
The handles of the plastic bag disarmingly
Smiling at no one in particular, or perhaps
At an invisible loved one, and you said
With a curdled edge of delight spreading
Through you, *Oh, that's such a beautiful sight...*

The Radio Man

Always wearing the same tatty pale blue jumper
The bearded Radio Man comes by and stops
To pat our dog, as he always does, and it doesn't
Even mind those loud static airwaves broadcasting
Constantly on that small transistor radio -
No doubt to drown out invisible voices
That try to spoil his day, or to avoid them altogether
With the right repelling frequencies -
Reminding me of some of my reading, of tea broker
Bedlamite James Tilley Matthews' persecutory
Delusions, first recorded case of paranoid
Schizophrenia, and of Viktor Tausk's thesis
On the influencing machine... The Radio Man,
As we call him, is clearly not entirely there,
Is always alone, always immersed in his own world,
And who can blame him, he has the most
Enchanted eyes I've ever seen, childlike,
Full of wonder, beautifully charged with light,
Radiating, glinting light, eyes that are permanently
Beaming, brimming with kindness and innocence,
A man who has seen miracles, who perhaps
Has second sight, and yet most would recognise
He mustn't be quite right, must have mental issues,
Ones which would normally inflict much suffering,
And yet he always seems in his merry little world,
Cheeks flushed red, face of an enraptured tramp
Painted in kitsch acrylics escaped from his frame,
Blissfully free, heartful and effortless, funny
Suffering, if his life is painful why's he smiling...?

Damaged Gods

The gods are too worried to listen to us,
They are too preoccupied to hear our prayers
Long shut their mouths to the shouting of ours,
Something long ago took hold of them
And has gripped them ever since,
Warped their brows and shadowed their eyes,
Their expressions set like stone,
Ensconced in scouring introspection,
Stares fixed, unseeing except on the inside,
Stone-concentrating, sculpted out of their own
Scrupulosity, they are too concerned
With something other than their Creation
To give us their attention, hands clasped against
Their ears, lips mute, as if they are in shock,
Concussed from some terrible blow,
Some recumbentibus, or in inscrutable
Crisis piercingly silent, they chip away
At themselves thought by thought, they are troubled,
Tortured, obsolete deities, washed out by
Worship, wrung dry by religion, burnt-out
By offerings, marbleised by submission,
Traumatised by sacrifices they didn't ask for,
They are fraught effigies, fragile demiurges,
Gnarled with compassion fatigue, life-disfigured,
Fractured and liable to crack, a celestial
Tin of broken biscuits, impotent, used-up,
Long past their sell-by-dates, beyond repair,
They are damaged damaged damaged gods...

The Ghost of Elm Grove

Pale as a pit-boy, anthracite hair
Sooty against a soapy wax brow
Abstracted as the Black Country
That anchors you in gritted pasts –
But where does your gaze really haunt from?
Not that cramped Black Country,
Its cobbled backyards and etiolated lean-tos –
From a photograph perhaps, brought to life
Through sepia skin, tapering fingers,
Your marble lips' implicit misinterpreting…

I know those eyes, olive-coloured,
Moving through objects, seeing into people,
In turn denying their silent discoveries;
A soul mate I'd think you were had those
Such as us a need for them, haunted
By ourselves as we are; you daylight ghost,
I'll join you for a while in mutual haunting,
Trying to find our shadows long ago
Lost to the distracting light of others…

Cousin recluse, my unrelated sister,
You catch my soul in occasional glimpses,
When we both blink embarrassedly, stare away –
As if a moment of knowing one another
By look would cast off our disguises,
Leave us naked in the gaze of heartless
Observers; we must protect ourselves
With thoughts, writing, labyrinths of books…

The shelves of your sheltering fictions
Closet the autumn tones of an androgynous
Adonis you adore with platonic passion:
A poster blow-up of Keats' death-cast
Handsomely doomed by your Elektra-bed –
He, alone, and golden among male animas,
Flutters your heart; he, unspoilt by
Phallic grotesquery, an emasculated herm
In posthumous repose; an antlerless Herne;
Cropped on paper, castrated Romantic;
A genderless angel reigning supreme
Over your creaseless peach bed, absent
Aeneas to your abandoned Dido Shade…

I laugh to my bottomless soul in the light-
Relief of your toilet, wallpapered in poetry –
To perch on a loo-seat while reading Stevie
Smith, Emily Dickinson, Christina Rossetti,
Or whisper their poems in lip-clipped recital –
Only you could make defecation poetical…

On leaving, we kiss like siblings, so we are
Of a kind: kindred spirits… Behind the shut
Front door, as I move away, I see the white
Oval of your face slowly fade like a dimming
Fog-light, retreating back into the reclusing
Shadows of your sepulchral house –
A ghost blurred through the frosted glass,
An aspirin disappearing in cloudy water…

The Christ of Trinity Street

Dim grey November, I paused outside the old
Hulking industrial church, eyes hoisted up to
The tortured stone-wrought Christ twisted on
The cross, and scoured his aching look,
Could only speculate on the accidental
Symbolism in how the mauve-and-grey pigeons
Cooed and pecked at his crown of stone thorns –
Were these urban birds, these feathered
Roman familiars in empurpled plumage,
Iconoclasts or beaked sculptors? Somehow,
In this dark austerity, our so-called wealth-
Creators desecrating the welfare state,
Asset-stripping the last scraps of compassionate
Architecture and cooperative spirit,
Speculating up until the last penny of anything
Worth fighting for, but purely for profit
Rather than empowerment, a time when the spirit
Of justice is being mocked by the Pharisaic fetter
Of the law, it seems grotesquely fitting
That a roost of pigeons should be pecking
At the thorns prickling the curled scalp
Of a grey whittled Christ, as if to tap
The sharp points deeper into His chipped temples –
A flash mob of feathered atheists pecking
Amok in the violet strobe-light, these pigeons
Know not what they coo as they make their nest
In thorny stone… And further into town,
A hipster-bearded schizophrenic throws out
The money counters from the cash converters…

Scot of the Car Park

He's bedded in now for the cutting winter
Encamped in frozen eiderdowns and sleeping bags
Frostbitten eyes blinking through the slit
In his Balaclava helmet, he's almost as stiff
As a post at his outpost just off the high street
Part-insulated from biting winds
By iron bars that mark the boundary
Of the supermarket car park -that's his pitch,
Tent of tarpaulin, swears he's not outside alone,
That ghosts of old companions shadow
Him everywhere, ubiquitous at this altitude,
Shadows hovering through the snow
Of solipsistic shoppers in consumerist tundra -
He needs a pee but he's too cold to climb out
From his snowed-in dug-out, he knows
If he does he'll be gone for some time,
Could get lost, or be bruised blue as his lips,
Crushed ice to soothe the bumps, might not be
Able to find his way back, so best keep
The small plastic Union Jack fluttering
From the top of his crumpled mound before
It freezes over and is polished to an igloo,
An iced dome, a chill booth, a frosted tomb,
Him a frozen adult foetus inside a frigid womb...

Footprints in the Snow

My mother used to say when a Robin hops into your house
It does so as an omen forewarning coming doom
(For one of her grey uncles had passed away soon after
Playing enraptured host to such a rubecula visitor);
The Redbreast is a fleeting guest, a chat come unannounced
With unassuming friendliness, trusting in the gloom
Of winter, bringing colours, fire-brief orange, white and mouse-
Brown, seems to make itself at home in human room,
Its feathers quite unruffled under unfamiliar roof –
That there's nothing to fear in this sprightly portent's surely proof
That the darkening change it augurs gently falling soon
Like softly silent snow, is no more something to dread
Than a sudden change of wind, or the coldness of a bed,
Just brushing off a breath, or a through-draft with a broom,
In a moment, one of trillions that made us who we are;
Everything we think and feel and touch and love and know,
Our memories, experiences… footprints in the snow…

At Blake's Cottage, Felpham

Felpham, pelting rain, late December,
We turn the corner onto brambly Blake's Road,
And there, behind a low Sussex flint-cobbled wall,
Facing sideways to the pavement, crouched
Blake's Cottage, black thatch sloping over
Its roof like a vast sooty cat nuzzling into slumber,
Red-brick chimney-piece tall and straight
Against grey stone side, and below, a black
Wood door latched silent in its histories,
And a small blue plaque at the edge to the hidden
Front reading WILLIAM BLAKE, ARTIST, POET,
MYSTIC, LIVED HERE 1800-1803…
If only he were still residing there that grim
Day's pilgrimage, how much I'd have relished
Meeting him face to face, to capture at a glance
The unclouded wonder of that skyward stare,
Light-struck, inspired, inspirited, that saw through
Material things, *into* things, everywhere,
Visions and insights brimming in the glints
Of his blue-imbued slate eyes; to think he is
Rumoured to have composed *'Je-ru-sa-lem'*
Inside this unassuming cottage, hunched
Over his manuscript as his quill scratched those
Ecstatic lines to the soft thud of a pendulum
Under dreaming beams; how I wished to knock
On that black latched door and be met by his
Enraptured face, thank him for opening
My mind to the power of poetry, for helping
Me from innocence through experience to some

Aphorismic scrap of acceptance, and unburden
All my troubles, heap them at his feet in piles
Of books, clothbound inhibitions, glimpse his
Sublime nimbus brow and borrow some of its bright
Numinousness to embolden my mental fight…

Satyr in Yellow-Rinse

I first encountered him on a dismal damp-papered Sunday
On the deserted promenade, he stopped me and asked for
A cigarette –as he lit it I noticed his skin was sulphur yellow,

Akin to the luminous jaundice I'd once witnessed on
The pelt of a self-injecting Glaswegian glowing
In the dark of a homeless hostel where I once hesitated;

But this tint, this stain, I ascertained on closer inspection,
Was noticeably blotchier, and corresponded to
The piss-yellow of his small crop of tight hair –evidently

Dyed the previous night, along with his head and skin –
Presumably accidentally, or serendipitously...? –
And entire body, detectably already tanned anyhow

Beneath this sulphurous rinse... His symmetrical brown
Eyes said without a hint of irony or objectivity,
'I'm the greatest human who's ever lived: no, honestly,

It's trite to say it but it's true: I invented the steam engine,
The pacemaker and the electronic motor-neuron
Mechanism directed straight from a synapse in the brain...

Do you want to know what else I've invented?' 'No thanks,'
I said abruptly, suddenly bombarded by last night's reading:
Maslow on grandiose thinking, R.D. Laing

On the natural rehabilitative processes of delusional
Psychosis, schizophrenic hallucinations –rough-hewn
Pathways minds besieged by the daily bedlam needs

Must grope along in order to regain at journey's end
A sense of rationality again... etcetera...I didn't want
To snub this yellow-stained inventor but I was irritable

With rainy winds and wanted to walk on for some distance,
Not for long, then walk back home again: conversation
Not on my Sunday agenda, least of all with luridly skin-

Dyed Satyrs; so I waved goodbye to my illustrious
Acquaintance as he sucked on his cigarette and hobbled
Barefooted and shirtless back to the obscurity

Of his genius; and I, to my bitterer end in the trapped
Dark and smoke of an over-priced basement flat,
My next poem waiting... The next day, my feet bartered

Their way along the pedestrianised shopping street
Of a stone's throw from my bricked hibernations;
Paralysed with plasticised nausea at the pedantic ATM,

I caught on the humid balm a refreshing peal of pipe-playing,
Harmonious, skilful, beautiful, not at all amateur,
But almost supernaturally apparent, like something

That just is and needs no explaining –spirit-lifting,
So I turned to see which form this pipe-playing Pan
Had assumed for this day's busked innings: there, tanned

Legs and bare feet splayed on the pavement, a cap
Of barely legal tender chinking beside them,
Was the same yellow-skinned Satyr I'd been cigarette-

Stung by the previous day, playing away, in thrall to his
Melodic propinquities, oblivious to his deforested
Surroundings, piping in the moment of flow, resplendent

In his sunning semi-nakedness as if languishing
In a drowsy summer arbour somewhere afar in
A magical Narnia of his own making... Today, I

Approached him, not wishing, again, to get caught in
Conversation, but then, neither did he seem to wish,
Enraptured by his own wind-enchantments; so I dropped

A spill of silvers into his cap and walked away,
Though only after having caught his steady gaze
And held it for a moment as it looked straight through me

As if I was transparent, some ethereal entity,
One of those indistinguishable sprites that disturb
His reveries occasionally... Curiously this

Identical forest sprite I'd encountered today didn't
Ask me for a cigarette this time, in fact almost seemed
To want me to vanish, as if I was cramping his style;

No threat of a sesquipedalian diatribe on his
Pioneering contributions to humankind,
No inventory of all his epoch-defining inventions...

But this time, in the absence of his grandiose claims,
I suddenly felt more convinced by them, and that as
Sure as shoes are coffins for the feet, shops the funeral

Parlours of the soul, and tramps the Atlases
Of the markets' shadows, this vulcanised Satyr *is*
Pan, Bacchus, Vulcan, Apollo, Bellorophon, Adonis,
And any other marginalised demigod he chooses…

Two Yellow Birds from Hyderabad

For Prakash Kona Reddy

Dear Prakash,
My far flung friend
From Hyderabad
Hindu-Catholic
Heartfelt socialist
Poet, academic,
Philanthropist,
Documenter
Of lower castes
And untouchables
In priceless poems
And magical prose,
You reinvented
Yourself for
The bookshelf,
I have never
Forgotten that day
You visited me
In Hove going
Out of your way
Before you attended
The conference
Up in the big smoke,
When you brought me
Beautiful artisan
Gifts crafted by
Impoverished hands

Of Hyderabad,
I still have those
Two exquisitely
Painted yellow birds
Sporting grey beaks,
Crested heads
And zebra-striped
Wings, perched on
A miniature tree
Textured like bark,
A nest in-between
Cradling two eggs
Strewn with dry grass
On its green plinth,
Which I've kept ever since,
Perched on a shelf
Yet to take flight...

Your Own Shadow

I will always be with you
Like your shadow,
I will be beside you in your worst times
And will make them worse for you –
I will be in your head
Whether you like it or not,
I will turn every thought against you,
I will be every thought that obsesses you –
I will obsess you,
I will possess you,
I will disown you,
I will own you,
I will be by your side every day, every night,
Every waking moment,
And even in your sleep,
I will occupy your dreams
And turn them against you
Until you believe you are going insane –
And I do all of this
Not out of spite or malice
But out of love,
Because I know what's best for you,
It's best for you to suffer
That way you will never grow complacent,
You will never take things for granted,
You will never settle or feel you belong,
You will never be still enough to put down roots,
You will never grow into your own skin,
You will come to appreciate

Silence, darkness, emptiness, sleep,
And long for nothingness –
You will always feel,
Always know,
There is something bearing down on you,
Something you cannot escape,
Your own shadow…

The *Patna's* Last Pilgrim

After Conrad's Lord Jim

No fear without imagination; ideas, principles,
Pirates of the mind, no more so than
That of a sailor's; one moment of death-fright
In realities of night more terrifying than blind
Doubts of day; one moment of what some call
'Cowardice' drove him first to save his own life,
One who dreamt of acting heroically
Should such a moment come upon him,
Then drove him to spending the rest of his life
Attempting to escape his past but thus
Condemned to that moment's mental repeating –
He could never escape his memory,
That crash of seawater which rocked him
Stone awake from his romantic picture
Of himself to the shabbier reality
Of his own mortal weakness, the waking fear
Of death, succumbing to temptation of self-
Preservation, taking a leap in the soaking
Dark from a merchant ship tipped to sink
Any minute, tug them all under in its suction,
Hundreds of pilgrims huddled below decks,
Impossible to fit them all into one lifeboat,
Thus abandoned, left to unanticipated depths...

Jump man jump!
Singing, *Jump man jump!*
Singing, *Jump man jump for life!*

All life, feeling, touch breaks out in his eye;
A land-lover's fever for fresh water springs –
Who mote it be so all measureless things
In the soul of a creature uniquely possessed
Of knowledge of its own mortality,
Hunted limitations, should spill out, be
Cast overboard, cast out, tipped upside down
And hurled upon the destructive waves...

Patna, Patna, Patna's the name
Curses obscurity for shameful fame...

In his eyes there still shines the Jewel
Of dormant promise postponed in time,
Destined to fulfil itself fatally
In sweat and mosquitoes of corrupted Eden
If not for our Fall's intervention;
The rest of his life a penitent pilgrimage
Of good and recklessly courageous deeds,
Escaping his past, hiding his identity,
But unable to hide it from himself
He'd ultimately reconcile his soul
Through self-sacrifice in a noble cause,
Personal redemption in personal extinction...

With guile and gunpowder this inoffensive,
Mild-mannered, unassuming man,
Tumultuous grey China seas for eyes,
Discovers again in himself something pure,
Chivalrous, true, unimpeachable
Delivering him from himself just in time:
'Tuan' his sacred title among the natives
Of a distant island, gifted him for his bravery

And service in freeing them from slavery,
"Lord' Jim' was his unassailable alias
As pure as Gentleman Brown's was impure,
Piratical, purposely ironic; Jim, a self-exiled,
Nautical Cane in search of a 'good name'
To scrub out the mark on his character,
The stain... *There she blows*: the thundering
Cloud from a blunderbuss –just time for
Pride to check left and right, then thud
To the ground like a landlocked anchor -
The soul of a sailor drowns on dry land ...

Feeding Martin Eden

No one wanted to know him while he struggled
To make it as a writer, putting all his figurative
Eggs in one basket, devoting every waking
Moment to his unlikely calling, days clattered
Away at his hired Blickensdorfer typewriter,
Turning down blue collar jobs, pawning clothes,
Rags and belongings, fighting in writing against
The cage of his barred class, ostracised by
Most who'd pretended to know him, even shunned
By kith and kin, *A prophet hath no honour in…*
And all that…; defamed as a loafer, all anyone
Could say to him each day -instead of greeting
Him- was *Get a job*, an echoing mantra garbling
Into one long gibbering shibboleth, parrot-call
Of some obsessing jobjob bird: *Getajob getajob*
Getajob getajob! 'Get a job! Go to work! Poor,
Stupid slaves… Small wonder the world belonged
To the strong. The slaves were obsessed by
Their own slavery. A job was to them a golden
Fetish before which they fell down and worshipped'…

Now that he isn't in need of feeding
Everyone's feeding Martin Eden

And when he was starving, going without meals
Sometimes for days at a time, subsisting
On tins while writing, writing, writing,
Almost alighting spiritually, no one so much as
Offered him a dime or invited him for dinner –

But since he had finally made it, broken
The mould of circumstance and accomplished sudden
And unexpected literary fame on the back
Of manuscripts he'd beaten out of himself
On empty stomachs and rationed cigarettes,
Rejected manuscripts piling up under his
Rickety writing table, his boomeranging cargo,
Doing the rounds of publishers at great expense
Of stamps and envelopes –when he imagined
Magazine editors and the publishers
Using well-oiled wringers that robotically
Opened up envelopes of manuscripts to flip in
Pre-typed rejection slips then automatically
Reseal them and return them to the senders'
Addresses, unread… Now every Tom, Dick and Harry,
Every society hostess and well-heeled family,
Every social circle of this half-civilised Hell
Of a corner of San Francisco invited him
To dinner of an evening, now that he had made it
As a writer, but not just any old writer,
An acclaimed and handsomely remunerated writer
Who could more than afford to clothe and feed himself,
And more besides, everyone was feeding
Martin Eden now that he had *A Name*…

Now that he isn't in need of feeding
Everyone wants to feed Martin Eden

And it had all been for that fatal infatuation
He caught like a sweating fever by pure accident
After visiting a cultured middle-class family
Who wished to show their gratitude for his
Having saved a young gentleman son from a mauling

In a rowdy part of town, that fatal infatuation
With that snatch of a higher '*altitude of living*'
He had tasted one fateful afternoon
And the vertigo he'd felt when encountering
The innumerable leather-bound books,
Their bulging spines heaped on the shelves
Of that Olympian home where he feared
His broad shoulders and clumsiness
Of movement might at any minute knock over
Some priceless heirloom, for this half-snatched
Rapture and glimpse of possibilities for
An utterly different and more fruitful future
For himself if he could just somehow cling
Onto this fast-rushing freight of beautifully
Furnished thought and polished speech,
Of luxuriating language, this fetching ketch
Of perfected tastes and appetites, cultivated lives,
Which would whisk him away to a Parnassus
Of polite etiquette and better manners,
Acquired tastes and exquisite sensitivities,
Ultimately, then only to strand him upstream,
A castaway from his own landlocked class…

Now that he isn't in need of feeding
Everyone's feeding Martin Eden

But by the sweated time he'd achieved fame,
And he was being invited to dinner by everyone
And anyone, it was too late, he'd lost his
Appetite, not just for eating –and now after
All that time fasting as he fought for recognition
On precious few cigarettes, now that he
Was eating again, something was eating him;

(Or you could be
Indian, Latin, from
Anywhere that has
A hotter climate),
Who ask you where
You're from, who call
Out to you asking
Where your hijab is,
Even though you are
Not Muslim but
Coptic Christian
A bitterly ironic
Quirk of fate, faith and
Difficult circumstances...

Does Bognor Cro-
Magnon Gammon
Man think as he
Licks Gum Arabic
Of how the substance
That makes his
Cigarettes stick
So he can smoke
Them is ironic...?

Glossary

Gum Arabic

zareba: (in Sudan and neighbouring countries) a thorn fence fortifying a camp or village.

daguet: French for brocket deer, referring to a form of desert camouflage.

fatigues: modern combat uniforms/battledress.

Osman Digna: leader of the Hadendowa in the Mahdist War (1881-1899).

"Scroungers": pejorative term used by many right-wing British politicians and newspapers (the red top press) to stigmatise benefit claimants.

"Corbynistas": pejorative term used to describe supporters of Jeremy Corbyn, much smeared and media-misrepresented Leader of the Opposition Labour Party (2015-20).

The Origami Man

brown study: old-fashioned phrase meaning gloomy or melancholy mood or daydream.

Department for Wasting Paper: a pun on the Department for Work and Pensions (DWP), the now notorious government department in charge of the distribution of welfare benefits, which has developed over the past decade into something more akin to policing the public purse on behalf of taxpayers rather than providing support to the nation's poorest.

entfremdung: estrangement (German) in the context of Karl Marx's theory of alienation in the capitalist work place.

The Blue, the Gray and the Brown

Yggdrasil: the Great Ash Tree at the centre of the world in Norse mythology.

Psychopompos: spiritual guide of a living person's soul to the underworld in Greek mythology.

Yahweh: the ancient Hebrew name for Jehovah (God) also known as the tetragrammaton, meaning the four-lettered name, since it was written with four consonants YHWH or JHVH though had two vowels inserted so it might be verbalised.

Brambling Damp Rampant

This poem makes extensive use of European heraldic terms:

stainand: or *stain* is a non-standard colour in heraldry, such as *murrey* (mulberry), *sanguine* (blood red) and *tenné* (orange or tan).

rebatement: the modification of a coat of arms symbolic of demotion due to misconduct

grimpant: climbing or rambling

tergiant: something showing its back

vambrace: armour guards for the forearms

brassart: an armlet or armband

vamplet: a round metal hand-guard on a jousting lance

dexter: The right side of a shield from the wearer's standpoint, and the left side to the viewer.

escutcheons: a small shield.

WRAG: Work-Related Activity Group, a grouping for those deemed too incapacitated to work but who are expected to prepare for work in the future in order to receive their Employment and Support Allowance! (ESA) from the state.

Mendelism: The principles of genetics, specifically of single-gene traits,! based on the work of Gregor Mendel (1822-84), a Moravian monk and! biologist who established the laws that are the foundation of classical! genetics.

Damaged Gods

Recumbentibus: a blow that knocks someone or something down.

Footprints in the Snow

rubecula: Erithacus rubecula (Latin), the European robin (redbreast).

Gum Arabic (Reprise)

Gammon: a pejorative term commonly used in the UK since the EU! Referendum to describe the typical angry (mostly white) right-wing! English voter who tends to be against immigration. The term actually! originates in Charles Dickens' *Nicholas Nickleby* in which a "gammon'! tendency' is ascribed to the robustly patriotic Mr. Gregsbury.

Acknowledgments

The International Times; *The London Magazine*; *The Morning Star*; The New River Press 2020 Yearbook; *Poetry & All That Jazz*.

I am grateful to the Oppenheim-John Downes Memorial Trust for an award which greatly eased financial pressures at the time of finishing this collection.

www.ingramcontent.com/pod-product-compliance
Lightning Source LLC
LaVergne TN
LVHW091121180726
843490LV00002B/904